BEN MOORE
14 Songs

Medium High Voice and Piano

First printing: March 2006

ED 4284

Eight of the songs in this collection were recorded on
All My Heart:
Deborah Voigt Sings American Songs, with pianist Brian Zeger,
released by EMI Classics.

On the cover: *Late Afternoon*, oil on canvas, 28 x 22 inches, by Ben Moore.

ISBN 978-1-4234-0846-8

G. SCHIRMER, *Inc.*

7777 W. Bluemound Rd. P.O. Box 13819 Milwaukee, WI 53213

www.schirmer.com
www.halleonard.com

BEN MOORE

The music of Ben Moore has been performed by many leading singers, including soprano Deborah Voigt, mezzo-soprano Susan Graham, tenors Jerry Hadley and Robert White, and four-time Tony winner Audra McDonald. Voigt premiered four of Moore's songs and reprised his encore piece "Wagner Roles" in her Carnegie Hall recital debut. In September 2005 EMI released Voigt's first recital CD, *All My Heart*, which includes eight of Moore's songs. *Opera News* wrote: "Eight songs by Ben Moore form the centerpiece of the disc, and their easy tunefulness and effective settings offer Voigt plenty of emotional range…the romantic sweep and dark urgency of Elizabeth Bishop's 'I am in need of music,' the gently lyrical 'In the dark pine-wood' and the richly internalized imagery of Moore's restrained setting of Keats' 'Darkling I listen'…a heartfelt and richly communicative recital." Moore's association with Voigt also includes a tribute to Montserrat Caballé commissioned by the Metropolitan Opera Guild.

Ben Moore's music spans many styles and genres, from text settings of great poets to comic material for cabaret and concert stages, many to his own lyrics. Robert White has performed Moore's setting of the Yeats poem "The Lake Isle of Innisfree" at numerous venues across the country and on international radio. In 2005 the Marilyn Horne Foundation and the ASCAP Foundation/Charles Kingsford Fund commissioned the song cycle *So Free Am I*. Set to the poetry of women authors, it reflects the experiences of women across centuries and cultures. Among several commissions from the Metropolitan Opera is his duet "We Love the Opera," which was featured on their radio broadcast on New Year's Day, 2005, as well as three songs for Met managing director Joseph Volpe's Farewell Gala in 2006.

Special comic material for opera singers includes "Sexy Lady" for Susan Graham, as well as "Wagner Roles" for Deborah Voigt. "Sexy Lady," which *Gramophone* magazine called "gloriously funny," is featured on the CD *Susan Graham at Carnegie Hall*, released by Warner Classics. In *The New York Times* review of Miss Voigt's Lincoln Center recital in 2002, of "Wagner Roles" critic Allan Kozinn called it "the clear highlight...a brilliant comic song." In 1999 Jerry Hadley commissioned the chamber musical *Henry and Company*, a four-character memory piece with a text by Barry Kleinbort set in small town America.

Born on January 2, 1960, in Syracuse, New York, Moore grew up in Clinton, New York and graduated from Hamilton College. With an MFA from The Parsons School of Design, he also pursues a career as a painter.

CONTENTS

PREFACE

The songs in this album were written over the course of about three years. Many of them are settings of poems that have attracted me since childhood. They are intended for the concert stage and may be performed in any groupings singers may wish to create. The texts, for the most part, are about love, but love in quite a wide variety of modes and orientations. Here are some brief notes on each piece:

"In the dark pine-wood" is the first of three songs in this album set to a poem from James Joyce's collection, *Chamber Music*. Unquenchable longing is beautifully expressed in this short verse with its carefully chosen images. Though my setting may have a certain gentleness, there should always be a keen sense of desire in the performance.

"The Lake Isle of Innisfree" was commissioned by the Metropolitan Museum of Art for the tenor Robert White in 2001. It was premiered there in an evening of new songs by contemporary American composers. The text is one of W.B. Yeats' most celebrated poems, which may be interpreted as a yearning for peace on many levels: in the world, through death, or within the "heart's core."

"I am in need of music" is a setting of a sonnet by Elizabeth Bishop. It is one of the few poems I know that speaks effectively of the healing power of music. The poem is not celebratory, but rather declares a deeply felt need for music that will act as a kind of spiritual cleansing. The return of the opening motif should be highlighted to signify the "magic made by melody."

"When I was one-and-twenty" expresses the poet A.E. Housman's ever-present theme of lost innocence in a text which on the surface is merely lighthearted and witty. My setting is jaunty and rhythmic but its modal melody is meant to convey the sadness of disillusionment.

"To the Virgins to Make Much of Time" is set to what may be the most memorable poem, among so many, with the injunction to "seize the day." Bearing in mind its familiarity, I chose to add a dash of irony—in falling chromatic phrases—in order to tweak the notion that a woman must have a husband.

"Bright cap and streamers," with text by James Joyce, announces an unabashed lustiness. The song can hardly be performed with too much zeal.

"Darkling I listen" is a setting of the sixth stanza of Keats' *Ode to a Nightingale*. It speaks of the wish for escape from a world of sorrows, and at the same time expresses the ecstasy of oneness with nature. I have set a sustained melody against a texture of continually undulating 16th-note figures in order to evoke a dream-like state of mind. This song, together with "I am in need of music," was written specifically for soprano Deborah Voigt.

"I would in that sweet bosom be" explores one of Joyce's recurring themes: that of unrequited desire. The phrases should be imbued with the kind of ardor that comes only when the love object is unattainable.

"The Ivy-Wife" is set to Thomas Hardy's delightful poem in which the speaker personifies an ivy plant longing to entwine a great tree—i.e., a man. The suffocating effect of this "love" seems to mirror Hardy's perceptions of women, beginning with his overbearing mother, and certainly in recurring situations in his novels. I have tried to capture the comic boldness of the poem's protagonist as well as her lethal possessiveness.

"The Lover Pleads with His Friend for Old Friends" is the most spare and contemplative piece in this collection. This is in keeping with Yeats' poem which, for me, is not an admonishment but a word of caution from one whose motive is nothing but love.

"This heart that flutters" attracted me with its extremely poignant sentiment: a lover asks why she should not offer everything to her beloved just as a wren stores all its treasures in its tiny nest, even though this love may last only a day. The recurring motif in the piano part is meant to express subtle anxiety and heartache set against the simple, tender melody for the voice.

"Annie Laurie" utilizes the familiar Scottish verse by William Douglas. It expresses the love for a woman to whom marriage is impossible. The 17th-century text has been modernized in several instances.

"The Cloak, the Boat, and the Shoes" is set to an early poem of Yeats' which, employing three beautiful images, argues for embracing the sorrow in one's life. The final section should be sung as quietly and tenderly as possible.

"On Music" is my response to requests for a piece that celebrates the value of music itself. I have conceived of it particularly as a song to be placed at the end of a set or as an encore. It should be performed simply and directly. It is meant as an affirmation especially to those who dedicate themselves to a life in music.

Ben Moore
February, 2006

BEN MOORE

14 Songs

to Marilyn Horne

In the dark pine-wood

James Joyce
from *Chamber Music*

Ben Moore

With tender longing ♩ = 58

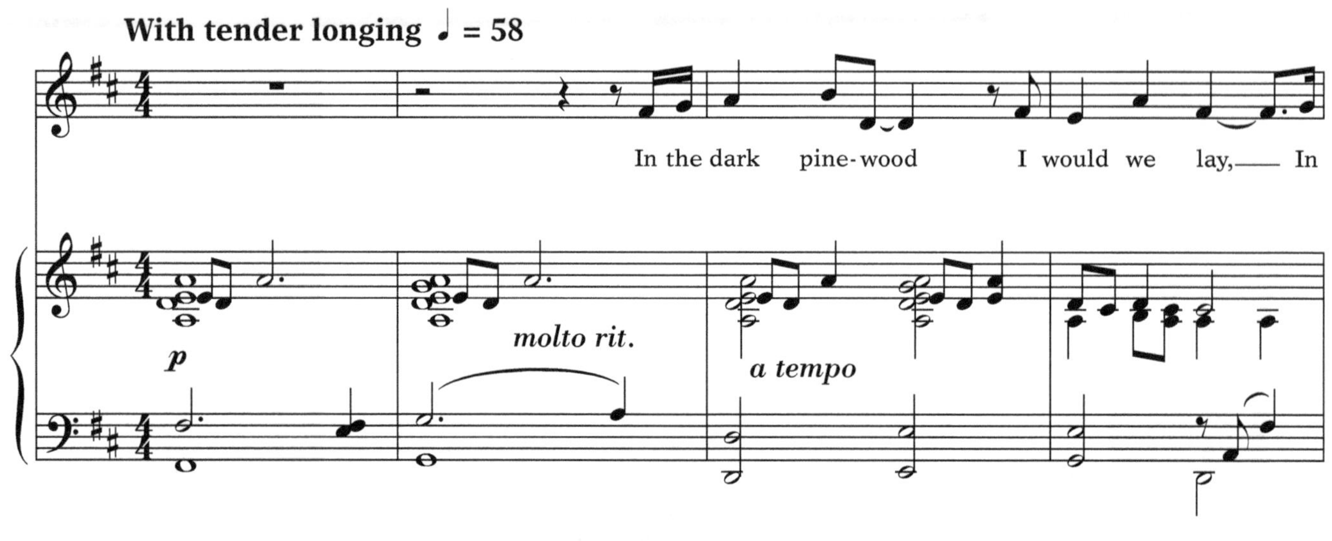

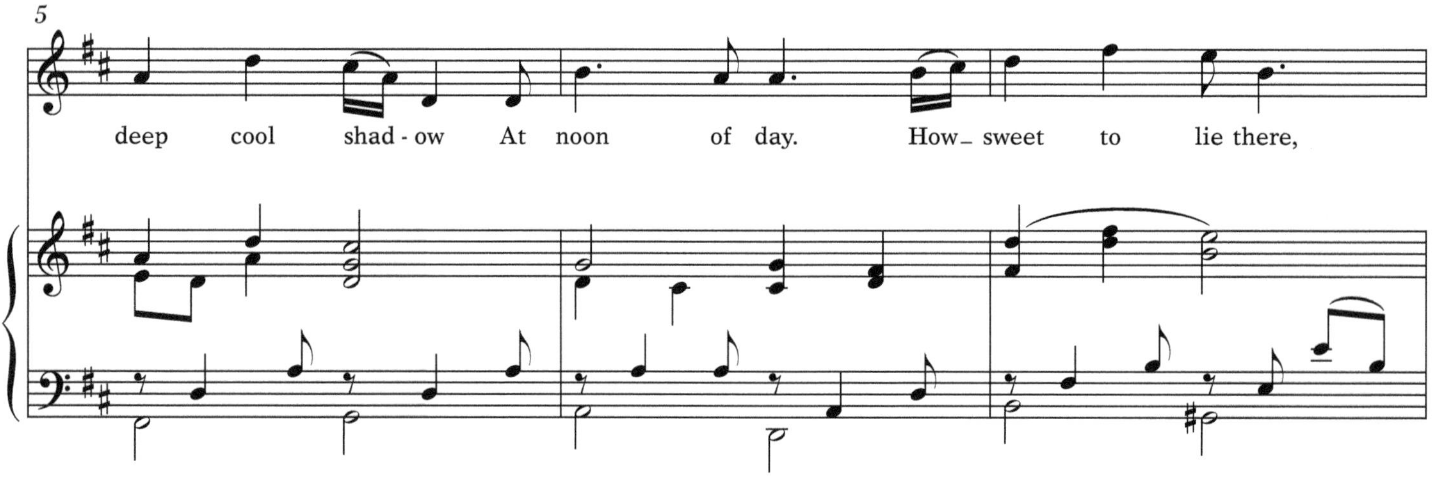

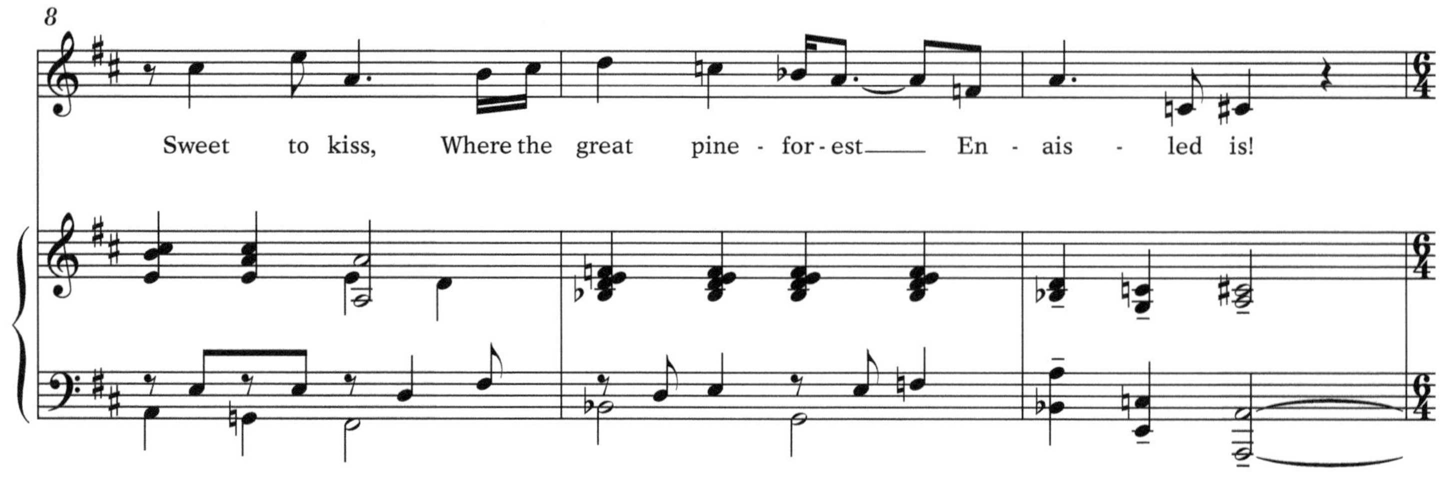

11
rit.
a tempo
Thy kiss de - scend - ing Sweet-er were With a
pp
mp
14
soft tu-mult Of thy hair. O un - to the pine-wood
mf
18
At noon of day Come with me
cresc.
f
21
rit.
now, Sweet love, a - way.
pp
p

for Robert White

The Lake Isle of Innisfree

William Butler Yeats

Ben Moore

5 *molto rit.*

Serenely, resolutely ♩ = ca. 88

p

I will a-rise and go now, and go to— In - nis - free,

Ped. ❊ Ped. ❊ *(Ped. ad lib.)*

10 *p*

And a small cab-in— build there, of clay and wat-tles— made:

14

Nine bean-rows will I have there, a hive for the hon - ey - bee, And

accel.
rit.
accel.
live — a-lone in the bee-loud glade.
p
p
rit.
molto rit.
a tempo
And I shall have some peace there, for peace comes drop - ping
p
slow, Drop-ping from the veils of the morn - ing to where the crick-et
mf
sings; There mid-night's all a glim-mer, and noon — a pur-ple
ad lib. r.h. (impressionistic)
mf

36
p
accel.
glow,
And eve - ning
f
p
40
rit.
a tempo
accel.
molto accel.
full
of the lin-net's wings.
45
relax tempo
rit.
molto rit.
Freely
pp
I will a-rise and go now, for
ff
pp
50
al-ways night and day
I hear
lake wa-ter lap-ping with low sounds
by the
pp

55
shore;
While I stand on the road-way,
or on the pave-ments grey,
I
60
mf
rit.
hear it in the deep heart's core,
mf
pp
cresc.
64
a tempo
rit.
accel.
rit.
the deep heart's core.
mf
p
68
accel.
rit.

for Deborah Voigt

I am in need of music

Elizabeth Bishop*

Ben Moore

*"Sonnet" [1928] from THE COMPLETE POEMS 1927–1979 by Elizabeth Bishop.

15
a tempo
fin - ger-tips, O - ver my bit - ter-taint-ed, trem - bling lips, With
18
f
p rit.
mel - o - dy, deep, clear, and liq - uid - slow.
f
p
22
rit.
a tempo
Oh, for the heal - ing sway - ing,
25
accel.
rit.
a tempo
p
old and low, Of
f
p

29
accel. poco a poco
some song sung to rest the tir-ed dead, A song
p cresc. poco a poco
33
to fall like wa-ter on my head,
37
rit.
And o-ver quiv-er-ing limbs, dream flushed to
ff
With a sense of arrival ♩ = 84
40
a tempo
rit.
a tempo
rit.
glow! There is a mag-ic made by
mf

44
a tempo
mel - o - dy: A spell of rest, and qui-et breath, and
48
rit.
accel.
cresc.
cool Heart, that sinks through the fad - ing col - ors
f
p
cresc.
As if submerged
51
a tempo
p
deep To the sub - a - que-ous still-ness of the
fp
l.h.
54
sea, And floats for - ev - er in a moon - green

57
mf
— pool,
Held in the arms of rhy- thm
mf

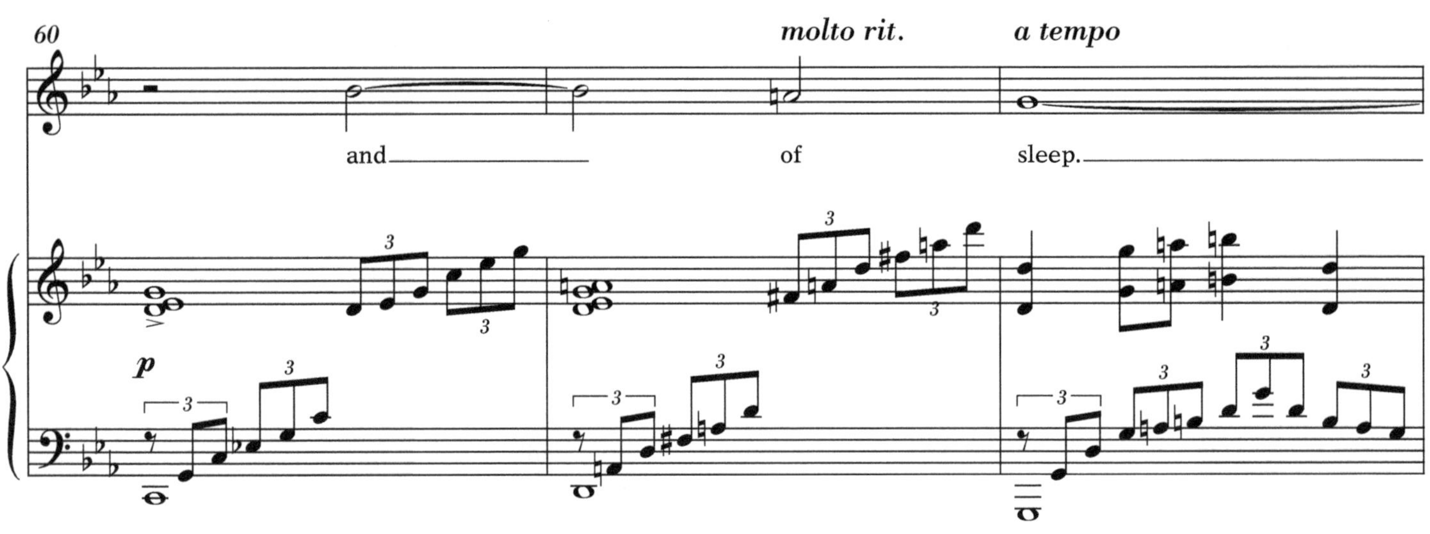
60
molto rit.
a tempo
and of sleep.
p

63
mf

When I was one-and-twenty

A.E. Housman
from *A Shropshire Lad*

Ben Moore

Vigorously ♩. = 120

f

5

mf

When I was one- and-twen-ty I heard a wise man

mp *f*

9

say, "Give crowns and pounds and guin-eas But

mp

12

not your heart a - way; Give pearls a-way and ru - bies But

f

16
keep your fan - cy free." But I was one-and-twen-ty, No use to talk to
mp
f
20
me.
24
mf
When I was one - and-twen-ty I heard him say a -
mp
27
gain,
"The heart out of the bos-om Was
f

30
f
nev - er giv'n in vain;
'Tis paid with sighs a-plen - ty And
cresc.
f
34
mp
sold for end - less rue."
And I am two-and-twen-ty, And oh, 'tis
mp
38
ff
true,
'tis
cresc.
42
true.
ff

To the Virgins to Make Much of Time

Robert Herrick

Ben Moore

13
rit.
mf
a tempo
The glo - ri - ous lamp of heav'n, the sun, The high - er he's a -
mf
17
mp
get - ting, The soon - er will his race be run And
cresc.
mp
21
near - er he's to set - ting. That
25
f
age is best which is the first, When youth and blood are warm - er; But
p cresc.

29
rit.
be - ing spent, the worse, and worst Times still suc-ceed the for - mer.
f
33
a tempo
rit.
a tempo
Then be not coy, but use your time, And
p
37
while ye may, go mar - ry;
For hav - ing lost but
41
once your prime, You may for-ev - er tar - ry.

Bright cap and streamers

James Joyce
from *Chamber Music*

Ben Moore

13
ten.
p cresc.
dreams to the dream-ers
That will not af-ter, That song and laugh-ter
ten.
ten.
p cresc.
17
f
Do noth-ing move.
f
ff
8ba
8ba
8ba
21
mf
With rib-bons stream-ing He sings the bold-er;
mf
ff
25
f
p cresc.
In troop at his shoul-der The wild bees hum.
And the
mf
f
p cresc.

30
time of dreaming Dreams is o-ver—
fff
pp
8ba
Ped.
34
p
As lov-er to lov-er, Sweet-heart,
39
f
I come.
pushing forward till end
ff
ff
43
47
p cresc.
ff

for Deborah Voigt

Darkling I listen

John Keats
from *Ode to a Nightingale*

Ben Moore

12
a tempo
rit.
a tempo
rit.
Called him soft names in man-y a mus - ed rhyme, To
pp
15
a tempo
molto rit.
a tempo
take in - to the air my qui-et breath;
18
Now more than ev - er
mp
22
mp
seems it rich to die, To cease up - on the
p

25
accel.
f
mid - night with no pain,
While thou art
mf
28
accel.
pour - ing forth thy soul a - broad
f
cresc.
31
In such an ec - sta - sy!
34
rit.
a tempo
ff
fff
p

37
pp
rit.
ppp
40
a tempo
p
rit.
Still wouldst thou sing, and I have
p
42
a tempo
rit.
a tempo
ears in vain— To thy high req - ui-em
45
molto rit.
a tempo
be-come a sod.
colla voce
cresc.
49
f
p

I would in that sweet bosom be

James Joyce
from *Chamber Music*

Ben Moore

13
rit.
a tempo
accel.
rit.
vis- it me. Be-cause of sad aus - ter - i - ties I
17
a tempo
would in that sweet bos-om
cresc.
Expansively
f a tempo
21
rit.
be. I would be ev-er in that heart (O soft I knock and
f
8ba
25
soft en - treat her!) Where on - ly peace might

29
portamento
be my part. Aus-ter - i-ties were all the sweet - er
cresc.
33
rit.
triumphant
rit.
So I were
ev-er in that
ff
36
a tempo
heart,
40
ev - er in that heart.
p

The Ivy-Wife

Thomas Hardy

Ben Moore

13
stretched an arm with - in his reach, And sig - naled u - ni - ty. But
17
p
with his drip he forced a breach, And tried to poi - son me.
p
f
f
21
I gave the grasp of part - ner - ship To one of an - oth - er
p
25
race— A plane: he barked him strip by strip From up - per bough to

29
base; And me there - with; for gone my grip, My
p
32
arms could not en - lace. In
mf
35
new af-fec-tion next I strove To coll an ash I saw, And
39
rit.
molto rit.
a tempo
he in trust re - ceived my love; Till with my soft
colla voce

42
green
claw
I cramped
and
pp
46
mp
bound
him
as
I
wove...
mp
49
mf
Such
was
my
love:
ha -
mf
52
ff
ha!
By
ff

Broader
55
this I gained his strength and height With-out his ri - val - ry. But
Slowly, freely
molto rit.
59
in my tri-umph— I lost sight Of af-ter-haps. Soon he, Be-ing
63
bark-bound, flag-ged, snapped, fell out-right, And in his fall
67
Fast
felled me!

The Lover Pleads with His Friend for Old Friends

William Butler Yeats

Ben Moore

This heart that flutters

James Joyce
from *Chamber Music*

Ben Moore

14
rit.
a tempo
draw a-part And hap-py be-tween kiss and kiss; My hope and
pp
mf
18
molto rit.
a tempo
rit.
all my rich - es— yes!— And all my hap - pi - ness.—
mp
22
a tempo
rit.
26
a tempo
rit.
a tempo
For there,- as in some— moss-y nest The
pp

30
wrens will— div - ers— treas-ures keep,— I laid those treas-ures— I pos-sessed Ere
p
34
f rit.
molto rit.
(freely)
that mine eyes— had learned— to weep.— Shall we not be as
f
37
a tempo
rit.
p
wise as— they— Though love live but a
mp
40
rit.
day?—
f expansively

Annie Laurie

William Douglas

Ben Moore

11
(freely)
— me her prom-ise — true. — Gave me her prom-ise — true — Which ne'er for-get shall I —
5
colla voce
15
accel.
a tempo
— And for bon-nie An-nie Lau-rie
f
18
accel.
rit.
mf
I'd lay me down and die. Her
cresc.
22
a tempo
brow is like the snow drift, Her throat is like the swan, Her
mf

26
face, it is the fair - est That e'er the sun shone on. That e'er the
30
(freely)
accel.
sun shone on And dark blue are her eyes
5
colla voce
34
a tempo
accel.
And for bon-nie An-nie Lau-rie I'd lay me down and die.
f
38
f
a tempo
Like dew on the dai - sy ly - in' is the fall of her fair-y feet And like
f

41
rit.
a tempo
wind in the sum-mer sigh-ing Her voice is low and sweet.
fz
pp
Ped.
44
p
And though we say good-
ppp (dream-like)
p
47
bye 'tis for bon-nie An - nie Lau-rie I'd lay me down and
51
rit.
a tempo
molto rit.
die, and die.
8ba

The Cloak, the Boat, and the Shoes

William Butler Yeats

Ben Moore

12
a tempo
mf
sight.'
'What do you build with
p
mf
15
f
sails for flight?'
'I build a boat for Sor - row: O
18
rit.
f
swift on the seas all day and night
Sail - eth the rov - er
f
21
rit.
a tempo
Sor - row,
All day
and
night.'
ff

24
molto rit.
a tempo
pp very soft and tender
'What do you weave with
pp
27
wool so white?' 'I weave the shoes of Sor - row:
30
Sound - less shall be the foot - fall light In all men's ears of
33
rit.
Sor - row, Sud-den and light.'

On Music

Words and Music by
Ben Moore

11
pains For both the lov - er and the love - less one.
14
mp
Fill your days with mu - sic, with
f
mp
17
ten - der, joy - ful song. Dream your dreams to
20
accel.
rit. accel.
mus - ic you'll help your dreams a - long.

rit.
molto rit.
a tempo
Makes no dif-f'rence who you are or where you're from,
There will al-ways be a song to sing.
Sing the clam-or of the cit-y with its cease - less
hum, Sing the com-ing of an-oth-er spring.
pp
cresc.
f

38
rit.
a tempo
ff expansively
Fill your days with mu - sic, with clear and pow-er-ful
rit.
ff
42
a tempo
song. Find your way through mu - sic, you'll find you can't go wrong, For
rit.
46
freely
rit.
a tempo
there with-in a sim-ple an - them,
(sweetly)
fpp
49
mf
ten.
a glimpse of life be-yond our eyes
ten.
mf
mf / ppp (dream-like)

52
— like wa-ter mir-ror-ing— the skies.
55
So let the mel-o-dy start,
Let mu - sic
molto rit.
a tempo, pushing forward to the end
58
fill your heart.
61
rit.